LUNAR ESCAPE

ACKNOWLEDGEMENTS

The first person I want to thank is Julia White Rogers (Mom). I want to thank my siblings, August S. L. Jones, Sam Paul Jones, Stephen L. R. Jones. I want to thank Kayla Powers Jones. I am thankful to Samuel R. Jones, Jr., Ayden Jones, Austen Jones, Autumn Jones, Uncle Richard Rogers, Rock Rogers, Russ Rogers, Uncle Steve Rogers, Stephanie Rogers, Stacey Rogers, and Mandy Rogers. The late Mrs. Anne F. Rogers, the late Leonard (Lennie) Rogers, the late S. L. Rogers, the late Samuel Robert Jones Sr., and the late Gladys Earline Jones are inspirations.

I want to thank my friends: N. Scott Reynolds, the best mentor ever; Nicholas Angelo Navatta; Angela Raschke Navatta; Pamela J. Navatta-Gregory; the late Angelo Navatta; Curt Navatta; Teddy Gregory; Benji Gregory; Barbara Williford; Rhonda Weyman; Justin Weyman; Erin Weyman; Robin Weyman; Victoria Williford; catherine

Doniel Smith Gaston; Eric Rowland, Nikki Carone Rowland, Kaylee Wilson, Emily Lengerich, Bobby Griggs, Dwain Paul Manor, Virginia Manor, Professor J. T. Callis, the late David Samuel Arnold, and the late Thomas Lawrence.

I want to thank those who provide medical care: Patricia Arns, M.D.; Nicole Hall, FMP-C; Jay Thornton, M.D;, Melissa Myrick, RN-C; Kelsey Taylor, D. O.; Kiara Dowling; Aladraine E. Sands, M.D.; Larry Brown; Sami Sivertsen; Kyle Wilson; Joshua Frierson; Shaun Womack,; Eleanor Layne Berlin; Gabriella G. Collier; Kara Stencel; Leah Marie Clem; Marissa Faye Wertheimer; Scott Harbin, D.D.S.; and Nathan Jones, D.D.S.

Finally, I want to thank the late Pope John Paul, II for inspiration.

MOON ESCAPE

CHRISTIE ELISE

JONES

Self-Published * Nashville

MMXXIV

Self-Published

Nashville, Tennessee

Copyright © Christie Elise Jones, July 2024

All rights reserved.

Without limiting the rights under copyright reserved above, no part of this publication may be reproduced, stored in or introduced into a retrieval system, or transmitted, in any form or by any means (electronic, mechanical, photocopying, recording or otherwise), without the prior written permission of the copyright owner.

For

Victoria Williford

Storm Systems Alert

Storm warnings are nice:
Beware of rain and
Beware of ice.
A gentle helping hand
During harsh conditions,
Confusing physicians,
Paying military attention,
A need for accountability,
Violence to surmount futility.

Only Wishes Allowed

Security at the Tennessee
Governor's house warned
That we were trespassing
And should leave promptly:

We were at the fountain
Making wishes, and we
Told them so, and we
Were permitted to
Make wishes,
And then we left.

Burden of Dogma

True without proof, this dogma,
Accompanied by a lengthy saga,
Full of riddle of some fact;
Truism to reenact
At the height of the Golden Age,
Presented by some sage,
Apologetics in high degree,
Reaching to agree,
Upon a national decree.

German Language and Me

I told some German girl
That I was retarded in German,
And if I give it a whirl,
We would determine
That I am a genius
In matters English.

Too Many Books?

With qualities connate,
Taking the same medicines
In a twinning state,
Into the womb, predischarged:

In a state of becoming,
With gender the same,
With the heart drumming
The twinning name:

If this is too many books,
Then so are the looks of fame.

Answers, Please

In the dainty high womankind
On the weather map,
Where prayers are undefined
And answers are in skullcaps,
As the children take a nap.

Horologe

Curled up and crying
In the Grandmaster's parking space,
Feeling like dying
To see his loving face:
The Grand Lodge
In the measured horologe.

Deep Learning

Deep learning in the shallows,
Keeping yearning in the hallows,
Where to go in the sea spray?
Exiting the vast Milky Way;
A spaceship may provide escape
For an intergalactic shipshape.

Ancient Puppets

O, sorry, we owe, we owe;
Putting on religious show,
Like Punch and Judy on a stick,
Children learn to laugh really quick:

A display of ancient puppetry
In a renewed pageantry;
Old puppets of the deep,
Cause for all to weep.

Promises

Entrusted in the ARMY
That none may harm me,
As a keeper of militant peace,
A wonder of literary release.

The ghosts of those long gone;
In occult we call on the bygone;
To labor in our sleep:
Promises to keep.

Dies Irae

On that day of wrath,
When the dead will rise
From the dire aftermath
Of ominous skies:

I shall call upon Jesus
As my only Savior;
My salvation superfluous
As well as good behavior.

Youngest

I was the youngest
On the Italian tour,
And my two coins
Were different
In meaning:
Two coins
For my own and
Another's return;
Not marriage,
For which I might dream
And the hotel, a carriage,
Closer to infancy it seems.
Fourteen.

Christian Soldiers

I might put up a fight
If it happens again;
My notes I will write
To my best friend:

Jesus works magic
At a godly will;
Prayers so thick,
Outcomes of thrill.

Tussle

I wrestle with a shadow
As a high of vanity,
With esteem of backflow;
Source of sanity:

Were I a brief alliance
Of a crucial T-square,
Taking needed sustenance
At a County Fair.

At Ease, Forever

Twins making a lifetime
Of mutual birthdays,
As a Christmas clock chimes
Through a daze of maze;
And the clock sends measure
In a ruler numbered treasures;
In a speaking, interactive portal,
Breaking free from mortal
Into infinite leisure.

Everlasting Peace

Magnificent state of peace,
Splendid ways of release:
Hallelujah, praise the Lord
With lofty song and soft sword.

Ancient Tasks

The imagination is fertile
For grounds of the inner circle;
The secret masquerade
In the hidden parade:
A ball of secret handshakes
And occluding courts;
Shadows dancing shapes
To ancient tasks exhorts.

Dude

Whoa, whoa, I thought that you
Were a dude, whoa, whoa;
I don't want to be rude,
But, I thought that you were a bro.

I get that a lot, and I feel
That as a dude I am hot;
I have been told to kneel
Like a knight's armor wrought.

True Knowledge

In the realm of conscious thought,
Conquer doubt and fear:
The battle that is fought
Brings forth immortal cheer.

What seems a waste of
Time or of dear money
May champion holy love
Like aged local honey.

For My Brother

A requiem for a brother,
A song of loving peace
Sung in the halls of hallows,
Where his spirit finds release,
Reclaiming his youth,
As it alone is the truth.

Poor Boy

That poor boy with a mower,
Poor, because he needs cash,
Also as a seed sower;
He is there in a dash.

Daddy did not teach him
How to delegate,
Or how to make a whim
The helm of saintly fate.

Whatever slipped by
As a stroke of genius,
As a forbidden high,
So heterogenous.

Hidden in the Pages

Ever so engaged,
The two sought privacy
And shelter in a page
Of reading primacy:

A sweatshop glorified,
On Christmas, sanctified.

A Ranting Lawyer

Let he who comes at my feet
Labor undetected, so discreet;
Cauterized vein of a *fabula,*
Singing hymns to a *radula:*

On the Day of Justice,,
Sink cold water in the bathhouse,
Desires of Emperor Augustus,
The Forum or thereabouts.

Mystical Words

Speak in holy peace:
Secretum petere;
Secretum dare, at least,,
The magic divinity;
The page has a crease.

What Chimbee Really Means

Chimbee, and I have no cuffs,
My Sensei prescribes katas to grow
And lots of knuckle pushups;
I, a child of the dojo,
Enjoy defensive fantasy
And well-behaved liberty.

Empty Glory Hole

Salve, I am the guard
Of this boneyard;
Sit here, and drink beer;
You have found favor deep,
With secrets to keep,
Secrets to keep.

Immersion, Latin and English

curalium vitavi cum in Mare Mediterraneum insilivi:
I avoided the curials when I jumped into the
Mediterranean Sea.

Immersionem magnum ludo erat:
Immersion was a great sport.

Risi cum curio maximus:
I laughed with the great court.

Growth

Solar traces on and atop
A mountain blushing,
A flower shop;
Scarabs hushing,
Yielding crop.

Squire

This irascible squire,
Giving the scribe a rise
And angering the choir
With holy war of surmise:

Guesswork, not clockwork,
Enraging the church bells,
Smattering the brushwork,
Opening a tome of spells.

Tiler

Where the needful Tiler dwells,
There is a book of spells
And an oath not forgot,
And a freedom that was bought:

Born in Blood, we are Brothers;
Accepting not any Others;
When strangers meet and approach,
I will refer to my solid oath.

Playtime

If Father Time could make baggage
For Mother Nature as an adage,
Self-contained in the brains
Of Lords, Ladies, and Babies,
With nothing to fear of Hades;

Then would the old-world
Laugh at the same time
As the afterworld
And find that it is playtime.

Cookies

That sweet Trefoil of Girl Scouts
Also tells the presence of radiation,
And a little girl who direly shouts:
"Let them eat cookies in this Nation!"

Broken Poem

It is a broken poem that we all know,
The thunder seeker of the big show;
Battalions forward in the station
Of wartime measured by generations:

Where did the honest clock go?
Stealing minutes of a shadow;
Rightly taking the whole stance
Of knowledge gained from ignorance.

Sweet Dreams

Is a sobbing, lonely damsel,
Ephemeral and unsubstantial
In a way and to the means
Of imagination to dreams:

With candy that is caught
By a baby who could not
Dream of another thing
That sweetness could bring.

Pompeii

Method of agape and eternal peace,
Singing triumphs and sleep,
Spirit to ultimately release
From ancient homes so deep,
And I weep.
That excavation of a population,
Mirrors and smoke in exclamation.

Money Issues

A shortage of money
Has caused mass hunger
And bankrupted the Easter Bunny
And shut down Santa's workshop:
The only food available is slop.

God Planted a Garden

Brought as soil for a garden;
The season did not care
If deeper there was oil,
For the fruits grew where
Two or more could share.

Giant Blastula

It is a giant blastula!
It is on the floor of my room;
It talks in nonsense:
Blatero, I babble,
It is blue and has nubs
For prime sensations,
For the start of love.

Kindness

Kindness is here;
May it not seem queer
That I would be so nice.
Let my words suffice
To be inspired by prayers
Of St. Francis of Assisi;
Here, there, and everywhere
Where the blind can see.

Recusatio, -onis, Feminine

Objection, Your Honor (s)
My client is being bombarded
With leading questions.

Sustained. Will the Prosecutor
Rephrase the questions?

Great Expectations

Another deep, abiding look,
Folding corners of a book,
Seeming like happenstance,
But nothing really is to chance:

Blooming in an environment,
Placebo of experiment,
Placenta of merriment:

Next. Birth. Next. Birth
Welcome to Planet Earth.

Wisdom

He is silent most of the time,
Startled when the clock chimes.
He raises a communion toast
In the presence of Holy Host,
Where the emptiness is Holy Ghost:
A bookmark for a Biblical plan,
A trusted advisor, a wise man.

Growing Stones

Where the stones grow statured
In an argument of rhetorical state;
Marvelous, they seem in dreams,
Magniloquent in their fate.
Who could ever make an equate?
A rate of attrition via division,
A work of love and of vision.

Remnants of the Holy See
Bring me out of captivity,
A tour of carrying a cross around,
Sheepishly making little sound,
Except for my headphones,
Bold, dire, and loud,
As my clan is Jones,
I need no shroud.

The Fall

Mirror, mirror, on the wall
Did the Roman Empire
Really fall?

The meter of a choir,
The gargoyles of desire,
Ancient humor high,
Ancient size of lullabies.

Mirror, mirror, on the wall
Did the Roman Empire
Really fall?

Chapel

Knowing that the Papal Chapel
Was not Eden's sour apple,
We prayed in the moonlight
For much more than a fortnight.

The mitre of the Holy show
Turned white in the afterglow
Of the radiant winter snow
From the balcony, down below.

Knowing that the Papal Chapel
Was not Eden's sour apple,
We prayed in the moonlight
For much more than a fortnight.

The Sword

A handsome, just reward
For confiscating a sword,
Duly bloodstained,
Further sustained,
Preventing attack
From a knight errant
In a terrible sack:
Standards of parents.

The Note

Noticed in passing,
A note of trespassing,
Solid state of fate,
Surpassing all late
Muses of the word;
First seen, then heard,
Literacy preceding action:
Liberty of satisfaction.

Lampoons

Anticipating any lampoon,
Enjoy intercontinental doom;
Have some peanuts on the way;
Try to find an ancient sleigh:

Fill your point with self-doubt;
Try to find your way out.

Hypnotic Oak

Mesmerizing pendulum,
So doubtful at behest
In the *querquetum,*
The oak forest:
The fallen oak strives
To greet as we arrive.

Truth and Consequences

I love to leave mistakes
For my beloved teacher;
I love to present sins
To my favorite preacher:

Rise and fall; fall and rise,
Take this way of truth
With sunny skies
As Sistine proof.

Really?

The obvious solution,
Removal of pollution,
Ill at ease with fits
Of massive wits;
It seemed to be a design
Of a fortunate mastermind,
Friend of humankind,
Trumpeting *silentium;*
Probitas, rectitude,
With a Papal Attitude.

Godfather

Papa is baby-talk for "pedagogue,"
Sometimes meaning "potato,"
Most often called "Father."
So, what do you know?

Any man at baptism
Can be godfather,
Bridging the schism
Of what could bother.

Turtle Soup

You are such a slow eater,
That you must eat turtle soup.
You are so approved by the pretor,
Outwitting your peer group.

An Old Map

It has a place on the spiritual map:
The trains of Scotland in deathtrap.
Taking to heart a dire condition,
Raising the bar of volition,
Reaching far back with petition,
Ready-made Christmas heliotrope,
Far away like unknown hope.

Classical Fantasies

In limitless possibility,
During the times
Of petty crimes
And of vanity versus charity;
And lots of room between,
Sea monsters on the scene,
Dreaming a place for Hercules,
In the Lotus Eaters' land of ease.

Deliverance

Deliver us from the medieval;
Grant innocence and peace.
From this slavery to sin,
Grant us full release.

He once was a baby,
Like everyone here:
Yes, no, or maybe,
Did you shed a tear?

Dry Erase Board

My dry erase board in my portal
Hosts many lessons as immortal
Truths of spiritual globes and all
With the prototype of a ball:

Do not reinvent the sphere;
Living or not, you are always here.

Wrinkles and Eternity

Insincere flattery aside,
You really get into stride
With the faces of places
And in between, spaces;
Making the grounds
For what surrounds
A wrinkle vanquished,
Forever anguished:
It will happen anyway,
Really, there is a someday.

Pirate's Ultimatum

Make ready for shore!
Man every oar!
Ride the hungry waves
That hurl watery graves,
Or face a fiery death,
Breathing your last breath.

Never Spooky

My little brother Booky
Is not ever spooky;
He predeceased me;
So, we will wait
To meet joyfully
At Heaven's gate.

Slow Drumming

Slow, steady marching
In an ancient arousal;
Torches light arching
Ceilings of arrival:

You are here,
And no more tears:
Your ancient heart
With a fresh start.

Redemption

Redemptio, I ransom,
From a collection,
Spiritual perfection;
And my redeemer
Knows why,
Instead of a vessel,
I fly.

Conscience

If it floats like a feather,
Why did it meet superego?
Drifting on foul weather
In a lush meadow,
Circumventing the sleeve
Of a suit of armor;
No need to weave,
I have my honor.

A Call to Arms

Strident commands and demands,
Filtered with echoing fantasy,
Approval and reprimands,
Beneath the tree canopy:

Rise up and take arms!
This is no false alarm!

Church and State

She taught that news camera
A hurried, yet thoughtful lesson
On the institution of a chaplain
And the revolution of caisson,
In underwater construction,
Equipped with instruction:
Baptism of a footbridge,
Without a bite, the midge.

Thirst

I have received
What I believed;
A summer tryst
Of morning mist:

What I give
And what I take,
For what I live,
My thirst to slake.

Iudicium Tenere

We won another case:
Time for victory pizza,
Sent to outer space,
Struggling in Venetia:

This telescope tells,
Like ancient church bells,
Of looking at the moon;
Nowhere is noon.

Palate of Speech

How to be polite
Without a bite;
Mastication aside,
Talking with food
Can be so rude,
As a way to abide.

Maritime Fame

As a method of delivery
Of seeming spontaneity,
Living out loud
In front of a crowd:

Fame was never here
As a beacon of hope;
The ship to be steered,
The story that was wrote.

Performance

I perform Handel's Messiah
To an Islamic audience, in Spring;
Feeling like a pariah,
Less the more I sing.

Neo-Linguistics

Neo-Latin and neonatal,
Babies cry and sigh
At the kitchen table;
A chair that is high
And a cake at their feet,
Humor so wry,
And measures complete.

Faith and Bones

Just as I was leaving
And left you all alone,
My mirror was believing
My inner facial bone.

Fitness

It comes as no surprise
That these headphones fit,
Made for 3-year-olds,
Possibly to acquit
A Cracker Jack prize.

Moll

This chair is for a doll;
That chair is too colossal;
This is for a moll:
A docile fossil.

Stylus

There is tech,
Then tech savvy,
Processing a check:
Ce la vie!

A stylus in the modern sense
Performs issues of expense.
Just ask at the scriptorum:
Why the moratorium?

Surprise: I care!

Why was he surprised
That I still have inspiration?
I was chastised and baptised;
Poetry is my vocation.

Christmas Gifts

It seems like a mess,
All of those unwrapped
Christmas presents,
Reaching to confess
Happy events:
This portal has contents
That are heaven-sent.

Wellness

No, we are not placing
Your daughter up for adoption.
Your son is going to be fine;
He is in recovery.
Your Mother is coming through,
And she is getting well.
Your Father is alright;
He put up a fight.

Grace and Cremains

Is it beauty to be sacred?
When place and space
Have the Bible read
And received grace,
What remains
From cremains?

Anchors Aweigh!

In the days of chain mail,
Still extant, we prevail,
Like a ship set sail
Where the ocean swells.

Walking through an archway,
Taking time to pray,
And to happily play:
Anchors Aweigh!

Moon Light

Ebbing, receding,
The moon makes way
Indeed, no doubt, proceeding
Looking like an ashtray.

The stars twinkle high,;
Like a worldwide lullaby
A child at a telescope
Aims at the moon with hope.

Ancient Arrangement

My visit to the Ancient Portal,
My stop by the Ancient Home,
Treats for the has-been mortals:
My origin is unknown.

I tell a tale of woe and sorrow
From the text of tomorrow,
Changing words in backflow,
Rearranging all that I know.

Thrust

Marching in flux and time,
Flowing to the sublime,
Knights Templar on the way:
Swords and ashes and clay

He thrust his sword in the ground
And vanished in the wind, early,
At the Ancient lost and found,
Not knowing an old tree's captivity.

Surgical Marginalia

I escaped from a surgery
Like an inmate from doom
Or a judge committing perjury
In a specialized room:

"Take it from me," said he.
"I know that you must flee
From the misfortunes
And margins of surgeons."

Contractions

An investment in a stylus,
A temporary silence
Of contractual liberty
Following pregnancy.

Really Old Currency

Known for the speedy purloin,
The state of consciousness
Profitless of wantonness,
Like an ancient prostitute coin
For positions of delight,
From a ghost in the night.

Part of Why I Am Roman Catholic

When the Roman Catholic nurses
Entered the hospital removing curses,
I listened and eagerly obeyed;
They helped me order dinner made
With high hopes and with deep prayers,
Helping me to get out of there.

Lay Assistance

I ate an icicle from a tree,
Because I was thirsty;
It crunched and melted,
And my uniform was belted:
Double outside belt and
Chain mail and command,
While the holy hourglass
Measures with dry sand
The laity of the early mass.

Bloody Salvation

While the body has many capillaries,
There are few feet, only two,
To choose from,
When *capularis* is the subject
Of one foot in the grave;
So, I will behave.

Merits

The converse argument of Value
Of Life as Repetition of Death
Affords the Absolute Necessity
Of Heaven for any Entity
Worthy of Existence
And of Eternal Distance.

Getting Older

Forty-five is a good age to be;
It is a landmark for me.
Forty-six is not so bad,
It is some of the most fun had.
All of the ages that are
In this book and the next
Are worthy of four gold stars;
No need for a complex
View of stars and bars;
No resorting to damned hex.

Vaping

Vaping is not a good idea,
Unless one plans to quit;
From depths of Pangaea,
Emerging as a half-wit.

Monsters

He is on a gondola asking why,
Acquitted by a hung jury:
Sententiis paribus absolvi,
To be pursued by Furies:

Not the same coils of Caduceus,
Offering three snakes, not salubrious,
Covered in hair so dubious,
To escape such fate, be studious.

My Great-Uncle

She says that every time I come there
That she is imposed to raise me;
Her husband is my great-uncle,
Who feels compelled to send me
To the Academy of West Point,
Where I learn proper behavior
 In a *scriptorium* pinpoint
And gratitude for the pavior:
I join the dream team as a Poet;
I am an Eastern Star, and I know it.

A Lullaby for Boo

When darkness draws nigh,
And Boo needs a lullaby,
She looks for her Mother;
There is no other,
My Immortal Mother has a machine
That catches every Roman Dream
And outwits the Grim Reaper,
As a little, cooing sleeper.

Audience Reaction

He could not act affably
And presented travesty,
Causing uncomfortable
Laughter and some tears:
An audience governable
By the addition of fears.

American Wishes

O were it actually true
That the red, white, and blue
Were the American hue:

Red for the blood that I pain,
White like the whites of my eyes,
Blue like my sacred veins,
Mixing up to make a sunrise.

Ministry

The restroom is in working order,
Ready for the harsh skateboarder,
Who has a tough sleep disorder;

Silent until she screams, tragic,
Informing the Ministry of Magic
With a swift barn owl
Of what is so foul.

Guess What!

Guess what I found out today!
I am definitely not gay;
To some that causes dismay,
It is true without delay:

Guess what I found out today!
My children are having birthdays
And existence days of child's play:

My vocation as a Poet
Is the reason that I know it!

Children at Work

Timbrels and soldiers on land
As the weave for father,
Who stays a mighty hand;
So, children it will not bother:

It is so! Tell me the blessing
Without second-guessing.

Ancient Sleep

It is written
In Classical Latin:
It has a page
Of a sage,
A saga deep
With Ancient sleep,
Here to keep
Beauty sleep.

Judaica for 5,000 Years

Someone replaced my
Hohner harmonica
With one approved by
And gifted to me by a rabbi
On Hanukkah.

Approval

If my Mentor approves,
Then that is all that I need:
If he notes that I improve,
I match words with deeds.

Wandering Downtown

I grumble and crumble
Up salt and brine;
Chinese mountains
Crumble into fountains.
I place a white carnation
On Saint Mary's Cathedral
Of the Sorrows of cognation,
A matter that is cerebral,
Celebration of nomenclature.

Precarious

We play word and image games
In the cold, large, stone room.
It is called the *scriptorium,*
Filled for a while with children's laughter,
The entrance note in this place is *precariium*
Obtained by prayer ever after.

Catacombs of Rome

I lit a torch to guide you
Through the maze of stones.
You say that if they need a clue
Then they need crossbones.

You slept in the catacombs,
Before you came home.

The Colors

From catatonic to
Hooked on phonics
As well as a view
Of what is new
In fashion hues
Like little boy blue.

Little White Lies

Let the babies get away
With their little white lies.
It is clever, so they say:
A gift that is small and wise.

Just Say Yes

He complains of the exit;
We care about what is said,
The parting gift from merit,
Possible to be dead.
He goes before me now,
Writing a book somehow;
Simple, yes, esculent,
Cibi, surely does vary,
When the party dines
As the dictionary,
For a way to marry,
With minimal tarry.

Isabella

She sought the door
Across the floor
Saying "Shh!"
To a noisy stone,
Leaping across
To gather home
Without a loss;
Intact bones,,
Especially the *patella:*
Call her Isabella.

Magic

The Craft of the Wise,
Herald of the Skies,
Yielding Sunrise,
And giving Sunset:
Not to Forget,
With no Regret.

Here comes the Moon;
Triquetra in tune.
The Gods bring Noon
Back as a nice Boon,
Sealed with a Rune.

Gina and Mike

She told me to do it!
I hid some cognac;
I made my own writ
Of *habeus corpus.*
Without attack,
Using wit:

I hid some cognac
Under a rock,
Kind of like Christmas
Without a sock.

Not Allowed

My Mother is not allowed
To ever be like a hag;
If she ever needs a shroud,
Then I would pack a bag
For the nearest station
For elation and elevation,
Into an SPQR machine,
To live a cheerful dream.

Understanding Harvest

Justinian understood
The impact of harvest
Between stone and wood;
Which one is very best
Comes at an election:
An Empirical Perfection..

Stern Flames

All Hallows' Eve,
If you believe
That you can return
To a bonfire stern,
Inspiring good behavior:
Ancient lore,
Refreshed pour
Concocted drinks,
As the Sphinx winks.

Mean People

You bring out the worst in me;
I really must admit
That you and eternity
Do not really fit.

Underage Law

We have greetings
On the voice command
Of legal proceedings
With underage reprimand:

Take that child away;
He is full of remorse.
If he were to stay,
It would be a course
Of a legal rocking horse.

Road Crews

Civil engineering
And criminal engineering
Are equated with work;
Machine Age rage
Makes roadwork
Berserk.

Safety

You are safe here and now.
You can rest here and now.
This bed is safe for you;
Take a softer, dreamy view.

This stone building has endured
Many outrageous storms;
Nothing that prayer cannot cure:
From worms to hellfire burns.

Candy Cane Lane

Hop aboard the stagecoach;
Sit and feel the rapt approach
To the cobblestone lane;
Enjoy the candy cane,
And give the horse alfalfa;
Bring along your pentalpha
And a lot of fun toys:
This ride is for girls and boys;
Make some happy noise!

My Friend

I have a special friend
From the Dark Ages.,
He is a true godsend
And we turn the pages.

If I have a fright at night,
He shows up in my dreams.
He comforts with torch light
And silences my screams.

Travel with Mommy

On my little way,
Mommy has me right;
Come what may,
Come what might:

I travel this road
Again and again
With my heavy load
Of toys for friends.

Thespian Surprise

In a full suit of armor, designed,
He seemed like a mortal threat,
With an ingratiating metal mind.
When he lifted his helmet,
They all did find spellbind,
Absolutely mind blowing,
On Broadway, it is showing.

International Friends

She has a lot of friendships
With kindness on their lips,
Willing to travel overseas
In order to surely please.
Now, that is a tall order
For any one as a boarder;
So, she takes in on kind
With a mind to be enshrined
In a library, not too scary.

Overdue

Check it out, without a doubt!
The books are in tall order:
The books for kids,
If they ever did
Have a childhood
With magick good
In a library so large
That it looks like a hoarder,
With an overdue charge
Of five hundred years
Causing a cessation of tears.

Words

I get so excited when I write;
So enthusiastic with all my might;
I love smithing words in ways
Pleasing to the eyes and the taste,
Not going anywhere with waste.

Delivery and Sleep

Out for Delivery,
Not too soon,
Nighttime imagery
By the light of the moon,
And of a mystery
Of silent victory:

Winning in sleep
Things to keep.

Static Interference

What a nuisance!
What is the origin?
Take a chance
To now begin:
Just say what;
And say when.

Medical Astrology

Along with standard medicine
And prayer for miracles,
Candles may attend
The ailments, and treacles
May invent heaven-sent,
Maybe to repent:
Certain cardinal directions
And witch's cake confections,
Offered at the consecrated altar
Not to waywardly falter.

Well-wishes

Deet. Boop. Goozle.
Cookie Monster Recusal.
Upon sworn perusal
Making a refusal.

Fantasy With Permission

Time, be still, not proud;
He sleeps on a cloud
Away from strife
With heavenly life;
Not to be hurt,
Away from dirt:

Hyperbaric chamber,
Bedchamber;
Oxygen therapy,
Obstetrics parity:

Rudolph the red-nosed
Reindeer
Flies in fantasy,
Not insanity.

Affection

I am tired of gaslighting;
I am bored with fist-fighting.
Maybe in some parallel way
I can change what I say:
Dimensions and algorithms;
Parties and schisms;
I need some direction
To pure affection.

Drama Class

All eyes on Aimee, or not,
Drama class in high school;
Her act is seven rages thought,
Little girl wet with drool:

Shoelace soup,
Easy doop
In a dream,
So obscene.

Sweet Dreams

Lollipop,
Jellybeans,
Candy shop;
Gumdrops,
Sock hop,
Valentine;
Toy shop,
Halloween.

Wisdom

To dare; to know,
To be silent;
A proven formula
For wisdom.

Daydreams and Moonbeams

The alpha state
Of daydreams
Can create
With light beams
Alternate fates
With what seems
Moonbeams
In the day:
A bouquet
Of moonflowers
After hours.

Some Questions

Which seed do I need?
Which book do I read?
Which book should I write?
To whom do I dedicate
This poetry of fate?

Ancient Pro-Life

The goddess of creativity,
Or Pallas Athena
Of ancient activity
And vena cava,
Returning to life
An ancient one,
Pro-life:
Tympanic drum.

Rain and Armor

The Knights Templar
Left a huge scar
On my soul in training,
While outside it is raining,
Shelter in the monastery,
And it seems scary;
So, I must be wary.

Time and Travel

Watch out for your reactions;
Do not leave a chance to fate.
When I met Andrew Jackson,
I was silent like a birthrate:
Little babies in ancient carriages
Trying to go home,
Cancelling out miscarriages
At God's Holy Throne.

Irregular Imperatives

Dic. Speak.
Duc. Lead.
Fac. Make.
Fer. Do.

Marrying Toys

For my ritual bath,
I choose rosemary.
For a primrose path,
I cannot marry.

I will marry Christmas
And all of my toys;
Not superstitious,
Occult noise.

Pay in the Family

I did not ask for much at all;
We were poor when I was small.
I only asked for a little doll
And school books every Fall.
I understood that our pay
Was not earmarked to play;
And that when we did pray,
It was always for someday.

Elmo

The code word for "chirrin,"
The code word for "children,"
Meaning "clean your speech,"
And "that is out of reach,"
The code word is "Elmo."
He is a friendly monster
To help children to grow;
Mommies can concur;
With the whisperer.

Candlelight

Silent sunset, followed by rain
And reason to earnestly complain;
Rainy days, please go away;
I like to write outdoors, too,
My ink spills out things so new;
I have reason to write
By candlelight, at night.

Spoiled Rotten

A whim of bodily constitution
With a decision of resolution:
Here today; gone in sorrow;
Some may play in time to borrow.

Many have plenty; some do not:
Hush, little baby, or it will spoil the rot.

Baby Blankets

When the moon dances
Across the dark sky;
When the expanse is
With the third eye;
I will cover you with blankets
And place you in baby baskets.

Here Comes Company

How can one with so much fame
Have such a lonely lot?
Such a school-known name,
How many books must be bought
To cross that ever threshold
Into the lucky stronghold
Where 4-leaf clovers dance
In the morning dew of chance?

New Cliche

Request your holy water today;
For it may be gone tomorrow,
With a new method of cliche:

Toddlers' cheeks all aglow;
With candy and toys in a sleigh.

High Seas and Marriage

It was a mystery to me,
Who I could marry
In the Roman Catholic Church
With a right of search
On the high seas:
Thank you and please.

Seal of Solomon Ring

My ring grows heavier
With each passing day,
When mailed with excelsior,
Meeting the intended with dismay:

I also have scrolls
For special people;
For whom the bell tolls,
And the silent steeple.

Leisure

May the fastest boat win
In a rowing team to begin
Leisurely activity at college;
A bastion of knowledge.

Hair Follicles

The lion's mane, so soft,
Bringing spirits aloft;
It may just be a toy,
But Caesar is not
Your everyday boy.
When fishing, he caught
An eager viceroy.

Caravan

Touche! Kudos to the young man
Leading a high caravan
With curtains for the Princess
And feather fans for her solace:
She would get nothing less
Than a body that is flawless.

A Trip to the Candy Store

The candy store is really for
Those who get the news;
Released from what was swore,
Canon law sweetly to recuse.

Dungeons

I can hear his reluctance
About rescuing my brother:
A summons for young nuns
To pray him out of dungeons:

His Kali swords where
Guns are not allowed;
Saint Peter's square,
Drawing a crowd,

360 degrees of square,
Four right angles and
A rare prayer
With some wedding band.

Water Birthing

If I call on Dominus with a prayer,
I know that He will really be there,
Where time slips into wishes' care,
Stones falling silent in a day,
Where a child is born in a font
To an exasperated Mother
Who knows better than to haunt
Where infantile longings
Find parental romance in romaunt,
Meeting the display of belongings.

The Calling of the Nun

She is a professional at
Being still and being silent.
"Tacite!," Says the teacher
To the ill-fated remnant
Of a loveworn preacher.
The priest hears confession
From the loudest ones first,
And the silent ones burst
With the calling of profession:
To be a nun of silent ingression.

Excited About Forever

So much to learn in this life;
I am pro-life even for wildlife.
I do need an afterlife, indeed,
In order to read more books
And to scribe in the scriptorium
With a garden for my green thumb.

Saint Brigid

Saint Brigid, pray for me,
I am here and lonely.
Will you stop by
While I cry
On a balcony in Rome
And guide me home?

My Favorite Monk

He holds me for centuries,
When I am afraid;
Years become accessories
To millennia of memories.
Though I cry some,
My tears are always met
By what I can become;
By what I cannot forget.

Travelling Bed

I just made my bed,
And it was a mess;
It went to my head,
And I shall confess:

My bed is full
Of outer space
And witchcraft
With a wand
Instead of a rocket;
Many days are spent
With money in my pocket
That I should give,
That the poor may live
With more ease and health;
Arriving as a bit of wealth;
Instead, they may look
At the library with my books.

Bookstore

The local bookstore
Went out of business,
As though I could want more
With a witness:
I have enough to read
For many moons;
Enough to read
In many rooms,
With helium balloons
To decorate
With less weight.

Retrieval by Mommy

She protects me from evil
Of many wild kinds;
Many times of retrieval
From ill-intended minds:

Suffice it to say
That she has
Her own way;
Her own paths.

Cathedral Mirrors

When I look into
The looking glass,
I seek a true view;
Forecasts of Mass,
Seeking only kind
Of likeness rhyme;
Fit like a puzzle,
A subtle tussle.

Nursery Audience

Wind and rain are contained
Like forces that are made
Like sunshine and shade;
Some far away ordained
Priest who entertained
An audience with a short
Attention span:
A nursery school Chaplain.

Me and my Shadow

It seems like forever ago
When I saw my shadow--
And one by candlelight
In a flickering show
Of what I may know
Of things that fright
Me in the night.

Rent

Never pay one's rent early,
Or one may leave in a hurry
With more than one worry.
It seems that dreams
Invite one with schemes
With all of the means
For absent-minded scenes.

Records

Forbidden records of
Occurrences obscene,
Classified whereof,
He knows what seems
In contrast with pristine.

Quantum Leap

With a rhythm of wisdom
And a partition of a schism,
And a kaleidoscope prism;
He leaps across the stream
Into a puddle while bubbles
Take stock of what to redeem
In a find of rubble extreme.

Moon Gazing

Moon gazing at midnight,
My imagination takes flight,
And the silver astral cord
Comes with an award:

What height is it so high
And singing a lullaby?
How old is the moon?
Looking like white dunes:

I could easily savor
A cheesy flavor.

Moon Mantra

My mantra grows tired
Like an old choir
Needing refreshment
For time well spent:

Take it to the top,
And do not stop;
Runaway truck
Getting stuck
In mountain sand:
What a band!

Memory of Bells

With a dash of panache
And a sprinkle of time,
The Wednesday of ash
Hears the bells chime:

We must not ever forget
That cause for regret:
To restore health, *Recurare*
To recover, *Recuperare*.

Indictment

Too much milk
And too much bread;
Too much to think
About too much drink;
Maybe water with bread
Would nurture instead,
Like some ancient
Prison cell arraignment.

Ancient Dishes

Lead poisoning was
A disease of ancient
Wealthy people
Who could afford
Dishes that had
Lead paint on them
Ironic. Madness.
A gift of the gods.

Classical Latin

Classical Latin after
Ascertainment can
Be entertainment,
After discerning
What one is learning.

Bottom Shelf

Knowledge on the bottom shelf
Is usually oversized in a library;
Too heavy for a mirrored realm;
Too stationary to be scary.

Victory Inquiry

Victory as candy cigarettes;
How could one ever forget
What it felt like as a child
To smile as one so wild
That it tastes so sweet
And could never mean defeat?

Dance Party

A kinder use of agriculture
Is the party hoedown:
Part chivalric culture
And some barbaric culture;
Eager to please;
Fields without trees.

Qualifications

Literarum censura,
Censorship of literature;
Fatuus, a fatuous fool,
To be duly sure
To leave the school.

Tibia

Lucky that on impact
Most of my body was intact;
I only broke and fractured
A *tiibia* on my left leg,
A *fabula* of epic fact;
Hit by truck,
While crossing the street;
A matter of luck
A quickness of feet
Jiu-jitsu is how I knew
To smack down
In this town.

Alcoholism

I do not have an alcohol
Problem, my own or
Somebody else's downfall
The subject is sore
So I shall say no more

Only Friend

When I left and ran off,
She was only one step from
Taking aim in order to scoff;
A tasty bit of gossip to come
Full circle, again, and again;
Jesus as my only dear friend.

Command

Only so we may free
The body in liberty
Like a rude symphony
With a credit to man:
Explosions of patrimony
In a summation to span;
Little babes and children;
A civilian pavilion;
A treat to understand
Military command.

Jail and Brownie Scouts

What in this wide world
Can give me back
The years unfurled
With a little slack
A year in jail
With Brownie Scouts
No incoming mail--
What was that about?
I could be bitter;
I could feel woe;
Or be a babysitter
For those who know
That they do not belong
And have not all along.

Careful, Now

With my stationery
I must be wary;
If it is not what it seems;
Hand-crafted cardstock,
Guarding yard stick;
A delivery quick--
It could make for a meltdown:
Overseas, please,
This time I shall write
Where angels take flight.

Safety in Songs

Sporadic hymns from a bard
In the Cathedral of the Incarnation
Stone so hard; stone so hard
With a font for ablation
I sang my best and had a witness
Nothing at the time to confess
Wrapping matters up so well
With "Away in a Manger" as farewell.

Ministry of Magic
For Pythia Parnassus

My dry erase board is used
To learn, to teach, to amuse:
A happy travelling classroom
With a boom of costume,
Merging shadow and sound,
Only staying on holy ground:
If you are late to class some
Ill-fated day in the magic kingdom,
One must apologize well.
If you forget your wand,
Then I will not tell
The Ministry of Magic
That you fail:
Just grab a stick, quick.

Coquetry

Please appease me here;
Please accost me there.
Ask my brother if you
May speak to me;
I have at least three
Brothers to answer,
I learned how to merit
Courage to alert
Without being a flirt.

Not Okay

No. Not okay.
Did you not learn
From Cain and Abel?
Sit a spell.
I will teach you well.

Homework

Lost in numeration
Was the value;
Gone from incantation;
Glad you had you.

The hidden tunnels
And passageways,
Making bubbles and puzzles,
A childhood maze:

Bring home your work,
And do not rest shirked
Of true responsibility;
Remain loyal to nativity.

Little William

I told Shakespeare
That I give him
Permission
To babble and
To shake a rattle;
He was tired
Of being old
And of being dead.

Knowing Me

My Mother knows like no other
My *modus operandi*.
My brothers know like no other,
When I play for keeps

I shout, and I pray
The whole day
Where love
Comes to shove.

Copious

He was too distant,
Although desired.
I am too extant
To retire:
I sing my way
To better days.

Gooey Mace

The shoe fit, and I wear it,
With glee like toothpaste
And electric gun or mace:
Too hard to see if haste
Would change his mind
And try to be kind.

Alone

In times past, I was scared
Of being alone,
But now, I find I fared
Well with zones
Of things to occupy
My lonely mind;
Things to savor,
Things to find,
A mastermind
Of flavor.

Soup Kitchen

Many moons ago
A scientific show
Made the headlines
And the soup lines;
Eager to dine;
Eager to inform;
And to adorn.

Looking Ahead

Minimum wage, low,
Unquestioned authority:
High chairs and teddy bears,
Priority of minority;
Ago, ahead, also, and then
A chance, a glance,
Higher ways of stance.

Perfect Fit

My yarmulke is saved
For my little brother's head;
My roads are all paved,
Leading to his bed:
Try as I may;
Try as I might;
Ending the day
Tucked in at night.

Warning

He warned me of jinn;
For this, I am thankful;
Devil-may-care enterprise;
Sistine Chapel, blue skies.

Made in the USA
Columbia, SC
12 March 2025

61e68973-30af-4963-a845-c42ac13b7933R01